Day and Night

William Anton

The sun is rising.

It is time
to wake up!

Now the sun is high in the sky.

It is noon.

Late in the afternoon
the sun is low in the sky.

Now the sun is setting.
It is evening.

Now it is night.
You can see the stars.

You can see the moon.
It looks thin for a few nights.

Then, night after night,

you can see more and more of it.

Finally, it is a full moon.

Sometimes you can see the moon
during the day, too.
But you will never see
the sun at night.

When the sun rises again,

the night is over.

It is time to start a new day.